HILLSIDE PUBLIC LIBRARY

3 1992 00189 2448

MAR 1 4 2012

W9-ATF-541

HILLSIDE PUBLIC LIBRARY
405 N. HILLSIDE AVENUE
HILLSIDE, IL 60162
(708) 449-7510

Civil Rights Movement
Plessy v. Ferguson

Hillside Public Library

Civil Rights Movement
Plessy v. Ferguson

Amos Esty

GREENSBORO, NORTH CAROLINA

A view of
Canal Street
in New Orleans,
Louisiana, circa 1895

Civil Rights Movement
Plessy v. Ferguson
Copyright © 2012 by Morgan Reynolds Publishing

All rights reserved
This book, or parts therof, may not be reproduced
in any form except by written consent of the publisher.
For more information write:
Morgan Reynolds Publishing, Inc.
620 South Elm Street, Suite 387
Greensboro, NC 27406 USA

Library of Congress Cataloging-in-Publication Data

Esty, Amos.
 Plessy v. Ferguson / by Amos Esty.
    p. cm. -- (Civil rights movement)
 Includes bibliographical references and index.
 ISBN 978-1-59935-182-7 (alk. paper) -- ISBN 978-1-59935-208-4
(e-book) 1.
Plessy, Homer Adolph--Trials, litigation, etc.--Juvenile literature. 2.
Segregation in transportation--Law and
legislation--Louisiana--History--Juvenile literature. 3. Segregation--Law
and legislation--United States--History--Juvenile literature. 4. United
States--Race relations--History--Juvenile literature. I. Title.
 KF223.P56E85 2012
 342.7308'73--dc22

                                  2011010175

PRINTED IN THE UNITED STATES OF AMERICA
First Edition

Book cover and interior designed by:
Ed Morgan, navyblue design studio
Greensboro, NC

Table of Contents

NEW ORLEANS, LA.
UNION STATION.

An illustration from an early twentieth-century
postcard of the old Union Station in New Orleans.
The former train station opened on June 1, 1892,
and was designed by the architect Louis Sullivan.

1

A Very Short
Train Ride

On the afternoon of June 7, 1892, Homer Plessy purchased a first-class ticket for a train headed from New Orleans, Louisiana, to the town of Covington, about thirty miles to the north. After buying the ticket, he boarded the train, took his seat, and waited to be arrested for the crime he had just committed.

Before the train left the station, the conductor came by to ask for Plessy's ticket. The conductor asked Plessy if he was a white man. No, Plessy replied. Once the conductor heard Plessy's answer, it was his legal obligation to have Plessy removed from the car. Under Louisiana state law, Plessy, as a black man, could not ride in the same railroad car as whites, and the first-class car, with its more comfortable seats, was reserved for whites.

When Plessy refused to move voluntarily, the conductor went to get help. He returned with a private detective, who arrested Plessy and took him to a nearby police station. The next morning, after a night in jail, Plessy appeared in court and waived his right to an immediate hearing on the charge of violating the Separate Car Act, the law that required blacks and whites to sit in separate railroad cars. After being released on bail, Plessy returned home. His trial was scheduled to begin several months later, in late October.

Plessy probably could have gotten away with his crime. After all, his skin was no darker than many people who were considered white. But he sat in the first-class car because he wanted to challenge the law and had no intention of traveling all the way to Covington. He was part of an organization in New Orleans made up of men who wanted to challenge laws that discriminated against blacks, laws such as the Separate Car Act. Plessy and his fellow members of the organization believed that the Separate Car Act was unconstitutional, meaning that it violated the United States Constitution and should not be enforced. The only way for them to overturn the law was to take their case to the courts.

The first step in that process was for Plessy to board the first-class car and wait to be arrested. The next step came in October, when Plessy had a hearing in a Louisiana court. On October 13, a lawyer for the state of Louisiana, Lionel Adams, submitted a written summary of the case against Plessy. Adams argued that the Separate Car Act was intended simply to reduce tensions between blacks and whites by keeping them separate while they traveled by railroad. Every state had the right to pass such a law, he said. After all, the law required that the cars reserved for blacks and whites be equal. So, the law treated everyone the same. Blacks could not ride in cars

A vintage train similar to the ones that were segregated in the 1890s

reserved for whites, and whites could not ride in cars reserved for blacks. Plessy had deliberately broken that law, Adams reminded the judge, and he should be punished for his crime.

Plessy was represented by a white lawyer named James Walker, who also submitted a written argument. Walker had been hired by the Citizens' Committee to Test the Constitutionality of the Separate Car Law. This was the group of men that had planned the protest. The organization had been founded on September 1, 1891, when a number of black professionals in New Orleans met and talked about ways to challenge the Separate Car Act. In his brief for the court, Walker wrote that the Separate Car Act denied Plessy his rights as a citizen of the United States. Under the U.S. Constitution, Walker argued, citizens could not be treated differently because of their race. Forcing Plessy and other black men and women to ride separately from white men and women was a way of enforcing white superiority, Walker said.

Two weeks later, on October 28, both sides appeared in court before Judge John Ferguson to make their arguments in person. At this point, Judge Ferguson was not deciding whether Plessy was guilty—the arguments made by Adams and Walker were about whether the case could proceed. It was up to Ferguson to decide if the case could continue. If the Separate Car Act violated the Constitution, as Walker argued, then the case against Plessy should be dismissed. If the law did not violate the Constitution, then the trial could move forward.

After hearing the lawyers, Ferguson stated that he needed more time to think about the case. On November 18, he finally made a ruling on the issue. The Separate Car Act was constitutional, he ruled. The case against Plessy could proceed.

Many whites in New Orleans celebrated the decision. In New Orleans in 1892, as in the entire United States, most whites tended to believe that blacks were inferior to whites. That belief had been one justification for slavery. For hundreds of years, until the end of the Civil War, most blacks in the southern United States had been held as slaves. When the Civil War ended in 1865, it was not clear how to integrate former slaves into southern society as free men and women. Since the end of the war, the relationship between blacks and whites had been one of the most important issues facing the country. Many whites were not ready to allow blacks equal rights, even if slavery had ended. Blacks had realized that they would have to fight for these rights, including efforts such as challenging the Separate Car Act.

Five generations of slaves are shown on
Smith's Plantation in Beaufort, South Carolina,
around 1862. Prior to the Civil War,
blacks had known little else but slavery,
and integration after the war ended was difficult.

After Judge Ferguson's ruling, one editorial in a local New Orleans newspaper stated that the decision should put an end to this challenge. It criticized the Citizens' Committee for wasting its time on a futile effort. "The sooner they drop their so-called 'crusade' against 'the Jim Crow Car,' and stop wasting their money in combating so well-established a principle—the right to separate the races in cars and elsewhere—the better for them," the paper argued. The paper did make one complaint. It said that it would like to see even more legislation to keep blacks and whites as separate as possible, including a law against interracial marriage.

Homer Plessy, James Walker, and the members of the Citizens' Committee were not surprised by Judge Ferguson's decision, but it was still a disappointment. They were ready for the ruling to go against them, and they were also prepared to take the next step in their fight—an appeal to the Louisiana Supreme Court. Once again, however, they knew that the odds were against them, in part because every member of the state's supreme court was white.

So when the state's supreme court handed down its ruling, it came as no surprise to Plessy's supporters. The court ruled that the Separate Car Act was, indeed, constitutional, because it applied only to travel within the state, not to travel between multiple states. The court argued that states were free to regulate travel and other business that took place within the borders of a state. The justices agreed with the argument Lionel Adams had made to Judge Ferguson that the law applied equally to both blacks and whites. Whites were barred from traveling in the cars designated for blacks, just as blacks could not ride in the cars reserved for whites. So because the law punished everyone equally, regardless of race, it was constitutional, the state supreme court ruled.

04887 THE CABILDO, (SUPREME COURT) NEW ORLEANS, LA.

The Cabildo (Supreme Court)
in New Orleans circa 1900

Once the state supreme court upheld Judge Ferguson's decision, Plessy had only one place left to turn: the United States Supreme Court. Walker and the rest of the Citizens' Committee hoped that the U.S. Supreme Court would issue a more favorable ruling than the courts in Louisiana, but they also worried that a decision against Plessy would set a precedent for the entire country that would make segregation the law of the land. The case was by now referred to as *Plessy v. Ferguson*, because Judge John Ferguson was considered the defendant in the case.

The case would not end quickly. It took four yours for Plessy's case to make its way to the United States Supreme Court. It was up to the Supreme Court to decide if the United States Constitution allowed states to pass laws that segregated blacks and whites. If so, then Plessy was guilty. But if not, the Separate Car Act was unconstitutional, and Plessy was innocent. Whatever the Court decided, its ruling would affect the way black and white Americans would live together for decades to come.

The Shadow
of Slavery

Homer Plessy was only twenty-nine years old when he boarded that train in New Orleans, but he had already lived through many important changes in the relationship between blacks and whites in the United States. He was born in March 1863, in the middle of the Civil War, which was being fought to decide whether slavery would continue in the Southern states or be abolished throughout the country. At the time the Civil War began, in 1861, there were about 4 million slaves held in the South. Slavery had existed for so long in the United States that, for hundreds of years, few white Americans questioned whether it should be allowed to continue. Because most white Americans had never known a time when slavery did not exist, they tended to believe that blacks were inferior to whites.

At one point slavery had been a part of life in the North as well. But in the late 1700s and early 1800s, Northern states passed laws that prohibited slavery. Even in these states, however, blacks were not treated as the equals of whites. In some Northern states blacks were not allowed to vote or to serve on juries, for example. Even those whites who believed that slavery was wrong often did not think that blacks were the equal of whites. Very few whites believed in racial equality.

A lawyer from Illinois named Abraham Lincoln was one of many white Americans who held mixed feelings about slavery. He believed that whites were superior to blacks, but he also questioned the morality of owning another person as a slave. In 1858, Lincoln ran for election as a senator from Illinois. Although he lost the race, the election gave him a chance to answer questions about his views on slavery. Some whites were afraid that he was too sympathetic to blacks. His opponent in the election, Stephen Douglas, represented the views of many whites when he debated against Lincoln. "I do not believe the Almighty ever intended the negro to be the equal of the white man," Douglas declared. "For six thousand years the negro has been a race upon the earth, and during that whole six thousand years—in all latitudes and climates wherever the negro has been—he has been inferior to whatever race adjoined him. The fact is he belongs to an inferior race and must occupy an inferior position."

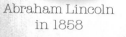

Abraham Lincoln in 1858

In his response, Lincoln told the crowd gathered to hear the speeches that he did not believe in social equality, either. He said that he did not know what could be done to help blacks in the United States. "Free them, and make them politically and socially, our equals?" he asked. "My own feelings will not admit of this."

But, Lincoln added, the question of how whites and blacks could coexist peacefully was a difficult one. He pointed out that slavery had long been a controversial issue in American politics, dividing Southerners who were worried that slavery would be abolished and Northerners who were afraid that slavery would spread to the North. It was not likely that the country would continue to have some slave states and some free states, Lincoln declared. At some point, he said, either every state would have to allow slavery or no states would allow slavery.

Lincoln did not win election to the Senate in 1858, but the race against Stephen Douglas did make him better known across the country. Two years later, in 1860, Lincoln was nominated by the Republican Party to run for president. The country was sharply divided in 1860, mostly because of differences resulting from slavery. The Republican Party had been founded in the 1850s by Northerners who opposed the spread of slavery. Most Republicans did not oppose slavery continuing where it already existed, in the Southern states, but they did not want to see slavery allowed in the North. By 1860, the Republican Party had gained many supporters in the North, but in the South, most whites were Democrats.

Whites in the South worried that Lincoln would try to abolish slavery if he was elected. Lincoln often said that he did not want to see slavery extended to the North, but he also tried to convince voters that he had no intention of ending slavery in the South. In the end, Lincoln won the election in 1860, but all of his support came from the North. In fact, he was not even on the ballot in ten states in the South.

The presidential election took place in November 1860. By the time Lincoln took office in March 1861, several Southern states had seceded from the Union because of worries that Lincoln and other Northern Republicans would try to abolish slavery. South Carolina was the first state to leave the Union, seceding on December 20, 1860. By early February, Alabama, Florida, Georgia, Louisiana, Mississippi, and Texas had also seceded and, with South Carolina, formed the Confederate States of America.

When Lincoln took office, he tried to reassure white Southerners that he had no intention of trying to abolish slavery. But a month later, fighting broke out when Confederate troops fired shells at a Union fort on an island off of the coast of South Carolina. Lincoln called for men to volunteer to join the Union army and put down the rebellion, which prompted Arkansas, North Carolina, Tennessee, and Virginia to secede from the Union and join the Confederacy. The Civil War had begun.

Both sides believed that the war would end quickly, but it dragged on for four long years. At first, Lincoln's primary goal had been to return the states that had seceded to the Union. But as the war continued, it gradually became a war to end slavery. On January 1, 1863, about two months before Homer Plessy was born, Lincoln issued the Emancipation Proclamation, which officially freed most of the black men and women held as slaves. The Proclamation did not apply to states where slavery existed but that had not seceded from the Union, or to areas of the Confederacy that were already under the control of the Union army, but it still applied to about 3 million of the 4 million slaves in the South.

THE EFFECTS OF THE PROCLAMATION—FREED NEGROES COMING INTO OUR LINES AT NEWBERN, NORTH CAROLINA.—[See Page 118.]

An illustration published in the February 21, 1863, issue of *Harper's Weekly*, with the caption, "The effects of the proclamation-freed Negroes coming into our lines at Newbern, North Carolina"

In his second inaugural address, in 1865, given after he won reelection, Lincoln acknowledged that slavery had somehow been the cause of the war, and that the war would determine whether slavery would continue. The war continued until the Confederacy surrendered in the spring of 1865. By that time, Lincoln and other northern politicians were already planning how to bring the Union back together and how to integrate millions of black men and women who had been slaves into American society. The first step came in January 1865, when Congress passed the Thirteenth Amendment to the United States Constitution. This Amendment banned slavery through-out the entire country. For an amendment to the Constitution to go into effect, three-fourths of the states also had to ratify it.

By the end of 1865, enough states had ratified the Thirteenth Amendment. Slavery had been abolished in the United States.

As the Civil War drew to an end and the Northern army gradually captured more territory in the South, the entire South faced the same question of how to integrate 4 million former slaves into the Southern economy without slavery. Whites in the South were not very happy to see slavery come to an end. The former slave owners had lost a free source of labor. Those whites who had not owned slaves now faced the difficulty of competing with blacks for work. Creating a society without slavery would not be easy, especially given that whites in the South had become accustomed to believing that they were superior to blacks. It would not be easy to change the way blacks and whites lived together.

In the final months of the war, President Lincoln drew up a plan to put the Union back together again after four years of fighting. The years after the war became known as Reconstruction because the federal government worked to rebuild the devastated South and to help ease the entrance of millions of former slaves into American society. Under Lincoln's plan for Reconstruction, if 10 percent of the voters in a Confederate state took an oath declaring their loyalty to the Union, that state would be allowed to organize a new state government and rejoin the Union. The new state governments would have to abolish slavery and create an educational system that would include black students, but states would not be required to allow blacks to vote. Lincoln hoped that by making the requirements easy to meet, he would be able to draw all of the states that had seceded back into the Union quickly.

Some members of Congress from Northern states felt that Lincoln's plan went too easy on the Confederate states. They wanted to ensure that the former slaves would be given more rights, such as the right to vote. Before the president and Congress could agree on a compromise, Lincoln was assassinated by John Wilkes Booth, leaving the issue in the hands of the vice president, Andrew Johnson.

The box in Ford's Theater in Washington, D.C., where Abraham Lincoln was assassinated by John Wilkes Booth. After Booth shot Lincoln he leaped on the stage from Lincoln's box, breaking his leg. As he ran from the stage, some heard Booth shout "*sic semper tyrannus*," which is Latin for "thus always to tyrants."

In 1866, Congress passed another amendment to the Constitution—the Fourteenth Amendment. This Amendment guaranteed blacks the rights of citizenship and forced states to respect those rights. The Fourteenth Amendment was necessary because several southern states had passed laws called black codes soon after the end of the Civil War that strictly limited the rights of blacks. Some of these laws barred blacks from voting or serving on juries; other laws prevented blacks from traveling freely or owning land. One Louisiana town passed black codes that required blacks to have a pass from an employer in order to enter the town, and blacks who did not work for a white person in the town were not allowed to live in the town. Blacks could not gather together for any purposes, even to have church services.

The Fourteenth Amendment made it possible to challenge discriminatory laws such as the black codes in court. If people felt that a law took away their rights as citizens, they could argue that it was unconstitutional under the amendment. Twenty-six years after Congress passed the amendment, Homer Plessy and the Citizens' Committee used it to test the constitutionality of the Separate Car Law.

3

Life in
Homer Plessy's
New Orleans

New Orleans was unlike any other city in the South, or even in the entire country. Traders from France had settled in the area in the 1700s, while the British colonies that later became the United States were all located along the Atlantic coast. Louisiana did not come under the control of the United States until 1803, when President Thomas Jefferson purchased a vast amount of land called the Louisiana Purchase from France. The purchased territory stretched all the way from the Mississippi River in the east to the Rocky Mountains in the west, and from New Orleans in the south to the area that is now North Dakota and Montana in the north. In 1812, Louisiana became the eighteenth state in the United States. Even after Louisiana joined the Union, however, French culture remained very visible in New Orleans.

At the time the Civil War broke out, New Orleans was one of the largest cities in the South. It was home to about 140,000 whites, 15,000 black slaves, and 10,000 free blacks. The city had always had a large free black community, and many of these men and women were of French descent.

The city was an important port for the South. Ships from around the world came to New Orleans to trade. Raw goods, such as lumber and furs, were sent down the Mississippi River from the American West, and finished goods were sent upriver on steamships to towns farther north. New Orleans was also a center of slave trading. Men who worked as slave traders brought their slaves to New Orleans, and plantation owners from all around Louisiana and Mississippi came to buy slaves. In 1860, young male slaves could sell for more than $1,600, and female slaves sold for about $1,400.

Given the importance of New Orleans to the South, it was essential that the Confederacy maintain control of the city during the Civil War. But the North also knew how important New Orleans was. By April 1862, just a year after the start of the war, Union troops marched into New Orleans and put the city under the control of the North. The arrival of the Union army immediately changed relations between blacks and whites in the city.

Unlike many other blacks in the South, Joseph and Rosa Plessy, Homer Plessy's parents, had never been slaves. But they had experienced the discrimination caused by laws that were meant to keep free blacks from becoming the social equals of whites. Joseph Plessy was born in 1822. Like many people in New Orleans, he could easily trace his ancestry to France. Joseph's father, Germain Plessy, had married a free black woman named Catherina Mathieu.

In the 1860s, during the Civil War, Joseph Plessy worked as a carpenter. Rosa Debergue—who became Rosa Plessy when she married Joseph—was born about 1835, and she worked as a seamstress. In 1863, Homer was born. By this time Union troops already occupied the city.

In general, free blacks in New Orleans had been quite successful, despite all of the limitations forced on them by discriminatory laws. Most free black men in the city were unskilled laborers, but some learned a skilled trade and became clerks, mechanics, shoemakers, or, like Joseph Plessy, carpenters. Many free black women worked as domestic servants in the homes of white families. A few free blacks in the city had become very wealthy, and in a few instances, even owned slaves themselves. Many free blacks spoke French, and some of the wealthier black families sent their children to school in Paris. The community that grew out of the mixing of French immigrants and blacks became known as Creole.

In many ways, Creoles in New Orleans were better off than blacks elsewhere in the United States. In the South prior to the Civil War, most blacks were held as slaves. In rural areas of the South, where most people made a living as farmers, there were few free blacks and many slaves. In New Orleans, however, there had always been a large community of free blacks.

Still, despite the fact that blacks and whites lived close together, passing each other every day on the streets, many public areas of New Orleans were segregated, including even the cemeteries. By law, free blacks could not vote, and many local businesses that were owned by whites either barred blacks from entering or had separate areas for blacks. Some theaters, hospitals, and hotels only served whites and refused entrance to blacks.

When Union General Benjamin Butler and his troops marched into New Orleans in 1862, it looked like it might be a new day for the city's black men and women. Butler allowed black men to enlist in the Union army, using them to

help defend the city from the Confederacy. The next year, on July 4, 1863, whites and blacks came together at an abolitionist rally, celebrating the end of slavery. Even before Lincoln issued the Emancipation Proclamation, thousands of slaves from all around Louisiana began to flee their owners. Many went to New Orleans because they knew that the Union army controlled the city. There they hoped to find freedom.

At first, the Union army built shelters for the newly arrived runaway slaves and provided them with food. By the fall of 1862, the army was helping to feed about 10,000 runaway slaves. As more slaves arrived in New Orleans, it became difficult to figure out how to provide them with food and housing. There was also little work for the former slaves, making it hard for them to earn money to support themselves. Some went to work for the army, but even the army could not make use of all the black men and women arriving every day in the city.

The steady stream of runaway slaves led to experiments in attempting to create a society that would function without slavery. Union General Nathaniel Banks came up with one possible solution. He knew that there were more black men and women than there were jobs, and he knew that some plantations in and around New Orleans needed laborers now that many slaves had fled. Banks decided that blacks who were able to work should be forced to sign contracts to work for pay on plantations owned by whites. The black men and women who signed these contracts would be allowed to maintain their families, to keep their own gardens, and to educate their children, but they were also largely under the control of the white landowners.

Some people—both black and white—believed that the system worked well. It provided plantation owners with the laborers they needed, and it gave former slaves a chance to make a living as free men and women. But many members

Union General
Nathaniel
Banks

of the free black community in New Orleans believed that there was not much difference between the system Banks created and slavery. Some black laborers were captured when they tried to leave their plantations and forced to return to work. They also received little pay, but they had to buy tools for farming from their employers, which meant that they kept even less of their pay. In short, the plantation owners were able to continue almost as if they still owned their workers.

An abandoned plantation house in
        Placquemines Parish, Louisiana.
Many plantation owners faced uncertainty without slave labor.

This system of labor did not solve the problem of how to create a more unified society in New Orleans. After the war ended, it still was not clear how the South's economy would function without slavery. Most blacks could not read or write, and they were usually the last to be hired by white employers—and the first to be fired if the employers no longer needed as many workers. White workers also resented this new competition from blacks and tried to prevent them from getting jobs that were usually held by whites. Many whites were surprised to find that blacks were resentful about having been held as slaves and that the former slaves no longer wanted to work for them.

Still, many blacks in the countryside believed that there would be more opportunities in New Orleans, and the black population grew quickly in the years after the war, reaching more than 50,000 by 1870. At the end of the war, the city was still under the control of the Union army, and, under the army's protection, blacks gained more rights than they had before the war. Local whites resented the presence of the army. In July 1866, tensions between blacks and whites led to violence in the city.

With the war having ended more than a year before, blacks in New Orleans and around the South wanted to make use of the rights promised to them in the new constitutional amendments. They also hoped to gain new rights, including the right to vote. Some northern politicians agreed that black men should have the right to vote, but others wanted to limit voting to white men.

In the summer of 1866, supporters of the right to vote for blacks gathered in New Orleans for a rally. In the days before the rally began, a local newspaper that was critical of giving blacks the right to vote printed rumors that the rally was really part of a plot to overthrow the local government. The paper helped whip up opposition to the convention. Whites who opposed black suffrage (or the right to vote) became angry that the meeting was being held. On July 30, a mob of white men prepared to stop the convention.

At about noon that day, the convention adjourned for an hour. At about the same time, a group of about two hundred blacks marched through the city's streets in support of the convention. They carried a United States flag and played music as they walked. Business owners in the area saw the marchers, and the mob, and began to close their doors, worrying that violence was inevitable. The crowd of whites drew closer to the marchers, and as the black marchers crossed one street, a white man pushed a black man to the ground. The black man got up and hit the white man. A white policeman saw this attack and shot at the black marcher.

As the marchers tried to continue down the street, other policemen began firing into the crowd. The marchers then tried to escape by running into the building where the convention was being held. The white mob and the police continued to attack the marchers and those who were attending the convention by firing shots and throwing stones into the convention hall. Some inside the convention hall tried to escape out a back door, but they found more angry white men there waiting for them.

The riot continued for hours, finally subsiding around 3:30 in the afternoon. In all, thirty-four black men were killed and another 119 wounded. One man was stabbed to death by a crowd of white men with knives. The police responded by arresting more than two hundred blacks, but they arrested only four whites. The next day, the local newspaper blamed blacks for instigating the riot.

Over the next year, confrontations between blacks and whites continued, as whites tried to keep things the way they were before the Civil War and blacks tried to seize the rights they felt they deserved. One cause of resentment among blacks was the segregation of streetcars, cars that rode on rails and were pulled by horses or mules, ferrying passengers around the city.

For years, the streetcars had been segregated. Some streetcar companies had different cars for whites and blacks, and other companies refused to allow blacks to ride the cars at all. In 1865, with the city under the control of the Union Army, a Union general declared that the streetcars would be integrated, meaning that blacks and whites would no longer be kept separate. The general's order was struck down by a local judge, allowing the streetcar companies to keep the cars segregated.

On Sunday, April 28, 1867, a black named William Nichols forced the issue by getting onto a white streetcar and refusing to leave. He was arrested and thrown off the car, but the charges were dismissed. Nichols then sued Edward Cox, the streetcar employee who had thrown him off the car, for assault and battery. Streetcar companies did not want to have to deal with deciding whether or not to allow blacks on the white cars or with the threat of being sued. They decided that if a black person got onto a car, the car would simply stay where it was. A test of this new strategy came on May 3, when a black man got onto a streetcar. The car remained sitting. One by one, the white passengers began to get off the car, frustrated. Eventually, the black man also left the car and the car continued down the street, although by that time it held no passengers.

A late nineteenth-century photograph by William Henry Jackson of a horse-pulled streetcar in front of the Clay Monument on Canal Street in New Orleans

Hillside Public Library

The next day, Friday, May 4, a group of black men confronted a white streetcar, throwing bottles and bricks at the streetcar. One of the leaders of the group, Joseph Guillaume, climbed on board the car. The driver left his seat to try to throw Guillaume off, but Guillaume instead threw the driver off. Guillaume then took the reins and drove the car down the street until he was eventually caught by police and arrested.

Guillaume's arrest did not stop the riot. As the police came out in larger numbers, the crowds of black men continued to grow larger. Eventually the police hemmed in the mob, and the chaos, but the protests continued the next day. Two black women joined the effort by boarding a white car and refusing to get off. The driver refused to move the car, and the white

Downtown New Orleans circa the late nineteenth century

passengers got off the car. Eventually, the driver grew so impatient that he continued his route despite the fact that the black women remained on the car.

The confrontations grew more violent that afternoon, as a group of black men and a number of white passengers fought on a white car. Blacks around the city tried to board other white cars, sometimes meeting resistance from the white passengers. By Sunday, mobs of white men also began to appear on the streets, and some members of the mobs of both black and white men carried knives and pistols.

Eventually, the city's mayor took action. A large crowd of about five hundred blacks had gathered at a square in the city. Several streetcars sat nearby, brought there by blacks who had taken control of them. Mayor Edward Heath went to the square himself to try to put an end to the riot. He met with a number of black men and women and asked them to stop their protests in return for considering ending the segregation of streetcars. They agreed, and soon the streets had quieted.

Although blacks in New Orleans seemed to have emerged victorious from this confrontation by ending segregation on the streetcars, violence was more often used by whites against blacks in the years after the Civil War, as had been the case in the 1866 riot in the city. In Tennessee, veterans of the Confederate army formed the Ku Klux Klan. Soon there were chapters of the Klan in other states. The group's members terrorized blacks, as well as many whites, threatening, beating, or even killing those who they felt were too supportive of rights for blacks.

The Civil Rights Movement

In response to the widespread violence in the South, some members of Congress began to push the federal government to provide greater help for blacks. They argued that until whites in the South were willing to allow black men and women to assert their rights, the federal government would have to take control of governing Southern states. But President Andrew Johnson was reluctant to use the power of the federal government to help the former slaves. The conflict over this issue led to a showdown between Congress and President Andrew Johnson. Ultimately, this conflict determined the role the government would play in rebuilding the South.

4

Integration
and Segregation

President Andrew Johnson turned out to be more sympathetic to the former slaveholders than to the men and women they had held as slaves. He pardoned the men who had led the Confederacy, and he fought the efforts of Congress to enforce tougher laws in the South to protect the rights of blacks. His policies were criticized by many Republicans. They argued that the goal of the Civil War had been to end slavery and to ensure that blacks received the rights they deserved. What was the purpose of the war if the states that had seceded were allowed to rejoin the Union without changing the way blacks were treated?

President Andrew Johnson

During the 1866 Congressional elections, Republicans were able to convince many voters in the North that they needed the power to make more widespread changes in the South. As a result, Republicans won a large majority in the House of Representatives and the Senate, giving them the power to override Andrew Johnson's opposition to their Reconstruction efforts. The dispute between Johnson and Republicans in Congress resulted from differences in their views of the role of the federal government. Johnson did not believe that the government should do anything to help former slaves gain equal rights in the South. Republicans, on the other hand, believed that, if the federal government did not play a large role in the South, there was little chance that blacks would be given the rights they deserved as citizens.

Most white Americans, whether they lived in the North or South, believed that whites were superior to blacks and that blacks could never be their social equals. Republicans tried to convince white voters that they did not want to make blacks equal to whites, they just wanted to give them the same rights. Thaddeus Stevens, a member of Congress from Pennsylvania, strongly supported passing laws that would protect the rights of blacks. "Every man, no matter what his race or color; every earthly being . . . has an equal right to justice, honesty, and fair play with every other man; and the law should secure him those rights," Stevens declared in a speech to Congress. "This doctrine does not mean that a negro shall sit on the same seat or eat at the same table with a white man. That is a matter of taste which every man must decide for himself. The law has nothing to do with it."

With the help of Stevens and other members of Congress known as the Radical Republicans who supported black rights, Congress passed the Reconstruction Act of 1867, which took away the right to vote from many former Confederates and required the states that had seceded to ratify the Fourteenth Amendment and to create new state constitutions that would give the right to vote to black men. The Act also installed federal troops throughout the South to try to maintain order. In 1869, Congress passed the Fifteenth Amendment to the U.S. Constitution, which was ratified by the states in 1870. This amendment guaranteed black men (but not women) the right to vote.

These actions by Congress helped blacks in the South make progress in their efforts to gain equality. By 1877, hundreds of black men had been elected to state legislatures, and sixteen black men even won election to Congress.

In 1868, Louisiana prepared to create a new state constitution, as required by the Reconstruction Act. When the new constitution was completed, it guaranteed that all children, both black and white, had the right to education in public schools, and it gave black men the right to vote. That June, Louisiana rejoined the Union. Over the next few years, even with continued violence against blacks and efforts to prevent black men from voting, there was a lot of progress toward a more integrated society. In New Orleans, some public schools were even desegregated, with black and white children now attending school side by side. In 1870, the state removed the ban on interracial marriage.

Education was one of the priorities of blacks after the Civil War. Slaves were rarely taught to read and write, as slave owners believed that educating slaves might make them more likely to run away. As a result, in 1870, less than 40 percent of blacks in New Orleans were literate. After the war, blacks had founded private schools and demanded that black students be admitted to white schools.

During the Civil War, Union General Nathaniel Banks had also helped create a number of schools for black children while the city was under the control of the Union army. The large number of students made it difficult, however, to give each one a good education. Some schools had more than eighty students for every teacher, and the students might range in age from six to eighteen.

In the years after the war, northern organizations sent assistance to black schools in the South, including books and salaries for teachers. One New York organization established two schools in New Orleans that together had more than sixty students enrolled. The federal government also assisted in educating black students.

Many whites in New Orleans were unhappy with the education of black students. Before the 1868 state constitution mandated support for public education for both blacks and whites, the city of New Orleans had refused to provide funding

A late nineteenth-century photograph of a
black educator's home in New Orleans

to educate black students, and many local whites did not want
to start using public money now to pay to send black children
to school.

But integrating public schools was one of the most important goals for many blacks in New Orleans. Black parents were
happy to have schools created for their children, but they knew
that it would be hard to maintain support for those schools
unless black and white children attended the same schools.
They also objected to segregated schools because it was clear
that prejudice against blacks was the reason to keep students
separated by race. Perhaps allowing black and white students
to attend school together as children would lead them to get
along better as adults.

For many whites, however, the idea of integrated schools was simply unfathomable. They believed that blacks were so inferior to whites that it would be insulting to force white children to attend the same schools as black students. That inferiority, they argued, was natural, so there was no point in trying to create equality through laws that created integrated schools. Nothing the government did could make the races equal.

Some whites in New Orleans did not feel so strongly about segregated schools. After all, black and white adults passed each other on the streets every day without violence, so there was no reason that black and white children could not sit near each other in schools. By 1869, some schools in the city were finally integrated. Keeping them integrated, however, was an even greater challenge.

In 1874, an organization called the White League began organizing protests against integrated schools. The League called for parents to remove their children from integrated schools. In December 1874, several black girls requested admission to a school that had been an all-white girls' school. A number of white students demanded that the black students be refused admission. If blacks were admitted, the white girls declared, then they would boycott their graduation.

The next day, a mob of hundreds of white men forced the city's superintendent of schools to pledge that he opposed integrated schools. On December 17, another confrontation developed at the Central Boys' High School, where a number of black students requested admission. When white students barred their way, the standoff seemed on the verge of turning violent before school officials closed the school for the day. By December 20, the fear of violence was so great that the school board decided to close the schools until the next month.

When the schools reopened in January, they officially remained integrated. But many black students who attended schools with mostly white students skipped classes at first out of fear that they would be thrown out—or worse. Not until spring did enrollment levels return to normal.

At some schools, integration seemed to go smoothly, but there were clearly tensions in the classrooms. The white writer George Washington Cable visited one integrated school and reported on what he found. He wrote that the black and white students would look at each other angrily, or sometimes in tears. The teachers tried to keep the students calm, but the students could not help but be aware of the tensions between blacks and whites outside the school.

For several years, these integrated schools were the most visible sign of the successes of Reconstruction. If the city could keep these integrated schools open, perhaps future generations of blacks and whites would grow up sitting side by side in classrooms. But in 1876, changes in national politics made it difficult to continue this progress in New Orleans.

In 1876, for the first time since the Civil War, the Democratic Party had a good chance of having its candidate, Samuel Tilden, elected president. The race between Tilden and the Republican candidate, Rutherford B. Hayes, was very close. In fact, it was so close in several states that it was not clear who had won. So, early in 1877, a group of Democrats and Republicans met and formed a compromise: Hayes would be president, but Republicans had to guarantee that they would remove federal troops from the South and give up on efforts to protect the right of black men to vote. Without the protection of federal troops and support from Republicans in Congress, blacks were left vulnerable in the South. White Democrats took back control of state governments and put an end to efforts to promote integration and equal rights.

The disputed 1876 election had immediate effects in New Orleans. After 1877, schools in the city that had been integrated began to be segregated again, and there was now less support for public education. Those black parents who could afford it might send their children to one of the many local private schools. Other black parents decided it was easier and safer to send their children to black schools than to risk sending them to an integrated school. The schools black children attended generally were in worse shape than schools for white children, and many black children did not attend school at all.

With Reconstruction over, blacks across the South soon faced new legislation passed by white-dominated Southern governments that took away some of the rights they had gained since the end of the Civil War. In 1887, for example, Florida passed a law requiring railroad cars to be segregated. Other Southern states followed Florida's example. By 1891, Alabama, Arkansas, Georgia, and Tennessee had all passed laws requiring railroad cars to be segregated. These laws, and other similar laws that mandated segregation became known as "Jim Crow" laws. The laws were designed to keep blacks and whites as separate as possible. (The term "Jim Crow" came from a dance performed by a white performer that ridiculed blacks.)

Louisiana was no exception. As whites became able to dominate state and local politics again, they tried to undo the progress that had been made during Reconstruction. In an election held in 1878, the men of Louisiana voted to hold a convention in order to write a new state constitution to replace the one that had been passed in 1868. The 1868 constitution had prohibited discrimination in public places. When the new constitution was completed, in 1879, it left out any mention of prohibiting discrimination. The new constitution did not require segregation to be enforced, but it also took away the support of the government for integration.

An illustration of actor Thomas Rice made up
in "blackface" as the character of Jim Crow

In the years that followed, whites in Louisiana continued to try to take away the rights gained by blacks during Reconstruction. But the black community in New Orleans was prepared for a fight.

5

A Slap
in the Face

In 1890, the Louisiana state legislature began debating whether to pass a law that would segregate railroad cars. Not everyone supported the law. The eighteen black men who had won election to the state legislature led the effort to block the bill from passing. One black representative, a man named C. F. Brown, asked in a speech to the other legislators why any of them would consider passing a law that would discriminate against black citizens who had worked hard, raised families, acquired property, and participated in state government. He asked his fellow representatives to set aside their prejudices and honor their oath to the Constitution, which he believed prohibited laws that required racial segregation.

A group of prominent black businessmen in New Orleans also organized to oppose the law. They formed the American Citizens' Equal Rights Association of Louisiana, which they said would fight to protect the rights of black citizens. One of the group's first actions was to write a letter to the state legislature to make its case. "Citizenship is national and has no color," the members argued. They pleaded with the lawmakers to follow the golden rule: "That men should not do unto others what they do not wish should be done unto them." The group urged the legislature not to adopt laws that would treat people differently based only on the color of their skin.

Rodolphe Desdunes, a columnist for the New Orleans *Crusader*, a local paper owned and run by blacks, urged the legislators to vote against the law. "Among the many schemes devised by the Southern statesmen to divide the races, none is so insulting as the one which provides separate cars for black and white people on the railroads running through the state," he wrote. "It is like a slap in the face of every member of the black race, whether he has the full measure or only one-eighth of that blood." Desdunes pointed out that the law relied on a vague definition of race. If only one of a person's parents had been black, should that person be considered black? What if just one of their grandparents had been black? In New Orleans, there were many people who were considered black whose families had many white ancestors as well as black ancestors.

Unfortunately for those who opposed the law, many whites in New Orleans were strongly supportive of segregating railroad cars, including the editors of the New Orleans *Times Democrat*, a local newspaper. In one editorial, the paper urged the legislature to pass the Separate Car Act by arguing that whites should not have to come into close contact with blacks. "A man that would be horrified at the idea of his wife or daughter seated by the side of a burly negro in the parlor of a hotel or at a restaurant cannot see her occupying a crowded seat in a car next to a negro without the same feeling of disgust," the editorial said. The editors argued that the law did not actually deny black citizens their rights, because it forced both blacks and whites to sit in separate cars, so everyone was treated the same. In fact, the paper's editors wrote in another editorial, the law was not hostile to blacks at all. The law would help keep the peace by ensuring that blacks and whites did not come into close contact. It was dangerous for blacks to think that they could be the social equals of whites, the editors wrote.

In the end, supporters of the bill won the battle, and the law passed. The punishment for any person who tried to sit in the wrong railroad car was a twenty-five dollar fine or twenty days in jail. The law also penalized railroad companies that did not provide segregated cars. The companies could be fined up to five hundred dollars, and conductors who allowed the law to be broken could also be punished. Railroad companies also had to post copies of the law in their ticket offices. There were no exceptions for members of the same family, meaning that if a white man and a black woman were married, for example, they would have to travel separately. The only exception the law allowed was in the case of black women who were hired by white families to care for children . Some railroad companies disliked the law because it forced them to provide an extra car for black passengers even if there were very few black travelers on a particular trip.

As soon as the legislature passed the law, blacks in New Orleans began to discuss how to try to get it overturned. One suggestion was that they boycott the railroads. That would mean refusing to travel by railroad as long as the railroads continued to segregate their cars. Another possibility was to challenge the law in court. On September 1, 1891, a group of black professionals in the city met to form an organization to challenge the law, the Citizens' Committee to Test the Constitutionality of the Separate Car Law.

Blacks in New Orleans had used the courts to challenge segregation before. In the 1870s, blacks filed a number of lawsuits against local businesses that refused to serve them, and they sometimes won in court. One black man even won a one thousand dollar settlement from the owner of a saloon for refusing to serve him.

The Committee held its first meeting at the offices of the New Orleans *Crusader*. The paper had been founded just two years earlier, in 1889, by Louis Martinet, and since then it had been an important source for the black community of information on political and social events. It was also the loudest voice in the state calling for equal rights for blacks. It was a weekly paper published on Saturday mornings. Shortly after the Separate Car Act passed, Louis Martinet, one of the leaders of the Committee, wrote in the *Crusader* that the courts could be used to challenge the law. He also urged blacks to avoid using the railroads in the meantime to try to put economic pressure on the railroads to oppose the law.

The Committee elected a local businessman, Arthur Esteves, as its president. For its vice president, the group chose Caesar Carpentier Antoine, a veteran of the Civil War. Many of the eighteen members of the Committee were among the elite of the black community, including a number of well-educated and fairly wealthy men. One member was a jeweler; another owned a funeral parlor. A few worked in government jobs.

The Committee decided almost immediately that one of its goals should be to challenge the law as soon as possible. The first step in the battle was to raise money to pay for lawyers to fight the law in court. Committee members asked friends and neighbors to contribute what they could to the cause. Within three months, the Committee raised almost $3,000 to cover expenses. With this money raised, the committee members now needed to find lawyers to help them challenge the Separate Car Act in court.

Louis Martinet asked a white lawyer from upstate New York, Albion Tourgée, to serve as one of the Committee's lawyers. Tourgée had gained some fame for his support of equal rights for blacks, and he had always been known for his independent thinking and his intelligence. He was originally from Ohio, and during the Civil War he fought for the Union Army.

Albion Tourgée

Soon after the war started, he joined a group of volunteers from the state of New York. It did not take long for him to see action. In 1861, he was wounded at the Battle of Bull Run. The battle was a great victory for the South and a surprising defeat for the North. As Tourgée and the other Union soldiers retreated, he was hit by the wheel of a wagon and knocked unconscious. When he awoke, he was at first unable to move his legs.

An 1862 photograph of Sudley Church in Bull Run, Virginia. Tourgee took part in the First Battle of Bull Run.

Tourgée returned home to Ohio to try to recover. With the help of a doctor, he eventually regained the ability to walk. As soon as he recovered fully, he returned to the Army. Once again, it did not take long for him to see action, and once again he was injured. This time, he was also captured by the Confederate Army. He spent four months as a prisoner of war before he was freed as part of a swap of prisoners by the two sides.

Finally, in December 1863, Tourgée resigned from the Army and returned to Ohio, where he studied to become a lawyer. By 1864 he had been admitted to the bar and was practicing as an attorney. When the war ended, he and his wife, Emma, moved to Greensboro, North Carolina. The Tourgées were among thousands of Northerners who moved to the South after the war. Some worked as teachers in schools for black children; others just saw good business opportunities in rebuilding the South.

Tourgée was one of those businessmen. He opened a tree nursery, and he also started a small newspaper, the *Union Register*. He became involved in politics and won election as a judge, but his outspoken views on race made him many enemies among whites in the area. He even began to receive death threats for his criticisms of the way blacks were treated, such as denying black men the right to vote.

Worried about their safety in North Carolina, the Tourgées moved to Denver, Colorado. Tourgée began to write novels about his time in the South. He became famous for the best-selling book *A Fool's Errand, by One of the Fools*, which was a fictional version of some of his experiences in the South after the Civil War. Although the book was fictional, it included discussions of racism and of the difficulties blacks faced in the South after the war. By 1891, when he was contacted by Martinet, Tourgée had written five more novels about the South during Reconstruction and lived with his family in western New York.

Martinet knew of Tourgée because of Tourgée's outspoken defense of the rights of blacks and his popular novels. Tourgée quickly agreed to help the Committee in its fight against the Separate Car Act, and he said that he would work for free. To help with the case, the Committee also needed to have a local lawyer in New Orleans, so they next hired James Walker, a white lawyer, who agreed to work for a fee of one thousand dollars. Walker had fought in the Confederate Army during the Civil War, but in the years after the war he had become sympathetic to the plight of blacks.

With the funds in place and two lawyers at hand to take on the case, the Committee was ready to start its battle in the courts. But first they had to find volunteers who would be willing to be arrested so that they could challenge the law. It was not enough for a traveler simply to be thrown off the train. Someone would actually have to be arrested and charged with violating the Separate Car Act. That would give the Committee the chance to argue that the law was unconstitutional and could not be enforced.

There were a number of questions the Citizens' Committee and its lawyers had to consider before moving ahead with their challenge. One question was who would make a good volunteer to be arrested. Should the Committee try to find a man or a woman? Did it matter if the volunteer had dark skin or light skin? And, once the Committee settled on a volunteer, how could it be sure that the volunteer would be charged with violating the Separate Car Act? What if the prosecutor charged the volunteer with a different offense?

One of Tourgée's first suggestions was to find someone whose skin was very light. Tourgée thought doing so would point out to the courts that it did not make sense to pass a law restricting entrance to "white" railroad cars on the basis of race when some people who were considered black had skin as light as some people considered white. Martinet, who was the son of a Creole man and a woman who had been a slave, responded that he had light skin and actually found that he was able to travel throughout the city without encountering any trouble because people did not assume that he was black. So, if the volunteer they chose had skin that was too light, it might be hard to ensure that the person would be arrested.

There was one part of the process that turned out to be not very difficult—getting a railroad company to help with challenging the law. The railroads disliked the expense of providing separate cars for blacks and whites, and they did not want their employees to be the ones enforcing the law. Martinet talked to the Louisville & Nashville railroad company and found that they were willing to help by having the first challenge take place on one of their cars.

L. & N. Station, New Orleans, La.—61

An illustration from a 1910 postcard
of the Louisville and Nashville Railway Station in New Orleans

The Citizen's Committee knew that it needed to make two separate challenges to the law. One challenge would be of the right of the state of Louisiana to enforce segregation on interstate travel—that is, on railroad cars that traveled from Louisiana to other states. A second challenge would be of the right to segregate railroad cars that only traveled within Louisiana. The reason that the two situations were different under the law was because of a clause in the United States Constitution that gives the federal government the right to regulate interstate commerce, meaning that federal laws apply to matters such as travel between different states. But, for travel within a single state, the commerce clause of the Constitution would not apply. So, it was possible that the courts would find that Louisiana could not require segregation on interstate travel but that the state could enforce segregation on travel with the state.

The Committee focused first on challenging the Separate Car Act in interstate travel. For its first recruit, the Committee settled on a twenty-one-year-old man named Daniel Desdunes, who was the son of one of the Committee members, Rodolphe Desdunes. On February 24, 1892, Daniel bought a first-class ticket for the 8:00 a.m. train traveling from New Orleans to Mobile, Alabama. Daniel boarded the train and took his seat in the first-class car, which was filled with white passengers. The train left the station, but two miles later, it came to a stop. Private detectives who had been hired as part of the plan boarded the train and arrested Desdunes, removing him from the train. Soon Desdunes was charged with violating the Separate Car Act.

As Desdunes waited for his day in court, the Louisiana Supreme Court issued a ruling in a similar case. The Texas and Pacific Railway had been charged with violating the Separate Car Act after a conductor on a train let a black passenger enter

A view of the levee in the New Orleans train yard

a car that was set aside for whites only. In its defense, the rail-road company argued that, because the black passenger was traveling to Texas, the laws of Louisiana could not force the railroad to provide separate cars. This reasoning was based on the commerce clause of the Constitution. So federal laws, the railroad company argued, not state laws, should apply to passengers traveling from one state to another. In late May 1892, the Louisiana Supreme Court decided that it agreed with the railroad's argument. The Court ruled that only the federal government could pass laws restricting the rights of passengers traveling between states, so the Separate Car Act could not be enforced in this case.

The ruling in this case meant that the Committee was likely to succeed in its case as well—Desdunes would probably not be found guilty. Less than two months later, on July 9, 1892, one of the Committee's lawyers, James Walker, contacted Louis Martinet with the good news: The local district court had thrown out the case against Desdunes on the grounds that the Separate Car Act could not apply to interstate passengers. The Committee celebrated the victory. Martinet wrote in the *Crusader* that Desdunes should be congratulated for taking a stand against the law.

Still, the ruling in the case of Desdunes was only a partial victory. The Court had ruled that the state could not pass laws requiring the segregation of railroad cars traveling from Louisiana to other states, but that meant that it might still be legal for the state to enforce segregation on cars that stayed within Louisiana. The Committee knew it had to challenge this possibility as well. And to do that, it recruited another black man who was willing to help, twenty-nine-year-old Homer Plessy.

6

Challenging
the Law

In 1892, Homer Plessy lived with his wife in an integrated middle-class neighborhood of New Orleans, where he made a living as a shoemaker. He had married his wife, Louise Bordenave, several years earlier, in 1888, when he was twenty-five and she was nineteen. They soon moved to a rented house in a neighborhood called Faubourg Tremé, which was known for its popular music halls. Both white and black families lived in the area, as well as a number of immigrants from Europe and the West Indies.

Plessy's father had died in 1869, but his mother had remarried two years later to Victor Dupart, a black man who was active in the movement for equal rights and who had a strong influence on Plessy. Dupart had six children from his previous marriage, and his first wife had died two years before he married Homer Plessy's mother. The family grew even larger when Victor Dupart and Homer Plessy's mother had a son, Charles, who was born in 1873.

Victor Dupart's family had long been a successful one in New Orleans, and the family included a number of shoemakers. In 1873, Victor Dupart joined an effort to bring together blacks and whites to fight for racial equality. Homer Plessy was influenced both by the political activism of the Duparts and by their success as shoemakers. He started working as a shoemaker in 1879, when he was sixteen years old. This was a popular trade among blacks in New Orleans at the time, but the era of small-scale shoemakers was gradually coming to an end as more as machines replaced human labor in shoemaking and many other trades. Working by hand, a shoemaker might be able to make just three pairs of shoes each day, which would make it hard to compete with faster machines.

Plessy was not as educated or experienced as many members of the Citizens' Committee when he agreed to be arrested for violating the Separate Car Act, but he was committed to the fight for equal rights. In previous years he had worked on trying to improve education for black students.

On June 7, 1892, Plessy had a chance to make another contribution. His train was scheduled to leave the station at 4:15. He boarded a whites-only car and took his seat. About twenty minutes later, after Plessy told the conductor that he was black, Plessy was arrested and taken to a jail in New Orleans's Fifth Precinct. There he was charged with violating the Separate Car Act. His trial was scheduled for October.

On October 28, Plessy appeared in court before Judge John Ferguson. Like Albion Tourgée, Ferguson was originally from the North. He was born in Massachusetts, which was home to the most active antislavery movement in the country in the years before the Civil War. He began his career as a lawyer in Boston, practicing as a private attorney. After the war, he moved to New Orleans, where he became a well known and successful lawyer. He had not been a judge for very long when he heard Plessy's case—since only that July, about a month after Plessy was arrested.

For the moment, the case would turn on Ferguson's decision. He had to rule whether the Separate Car Act was constitutional. If he decided that it was, then the case against Plessy could go ahead. If he ruled that the law was unconstitutional, then the charge would be dismissed. On November 18, Ferguson issued his decision. The Separate Car Act was constitutional, he ruled.

Walker, Tourgée, and the members of the Citizens' Committee were expecting the decision. As an article in the *Crusader* pointed out, given how rare it was for a black person to be treated as an equal under the law in the South, there was little chance that Judge Ferguson would have made any other decision. As a result of expecting the decision to go against them, Plessy's lawyers were ready to appeal the decision to the Louisiana Supreme Court.

They also knew that, once again, the odds were against them. Every member of the state's Supreme Court was white, including the chief justice, Francis Tillou Nicholls, a former governor of the state. Nicholls became governor in 1877, after the end of Reconstruction. Although Nicholls certainly did

Francis Tillou Nicholls

not believe in racial equality, he had at first shown some signs that he also did not believe in sharp segregation of blacks and whites. Louis Martinet had been impressed by Nicholls when Nicholls was governor, and Martinet wrote to Tourgée to tell him that Nicholls had seemed to treat blacks fairly as governor. By 1892, however, it appeared that Nicholls had begun to take a stronger stance against integration. So when the state supreme court handed down a ruling upholding the Separate Car Act, it came as no surprise to Plessy's supporters.

With the ruling of the Louisiana Supreme Court issued, Plessy and the Citizens' Committee looked next to the United States Supreme Court. Tourgée, Martinet, and the others involved in the case knew that a ruling against Plessy could hurt the cause of black Americans for many years to come. They had good reason to worry that the outcome might not be favorable to them.

In recent years, the U.S. Supreme Court had not been very supportive of the rights of black Americans. In 1857, the Court issued one of the most famous decisions in its history in a case involving the rights of a slave. A man named Dred Scott was a slave in the South, but his owner had taken him on trips north to the state of Illinois, which did not allow slavery, and to Wisconsin, which at the time was a territory, not yet a state, and also did not allow slavery. Later, after returning to the South with his owner, Scott went to court to try to obtain his freedom. He argued that because he had traveled to areas that banned slavery, he had legally become free while there and should no longer be considered a slave.

The U.S. Supreme Court decided against Scott in a decision that surprised many Northerners, both black and white, and pleased many white Southerners. Justice Roger Taney, the chief justice of the Court, wrote in his decision that Scott had no right to sue in the courts simply because he was black.

A painting of Dred Scott by Louis Schultze

The question, Taney wrote, was whether a black American could ever be considered a citizen of the United States. To answer that question, Taney offered his own interpretation of the intentions of the men who had written the Constitution. At the time the Constitution was written, Taney argued, blacks were considered inferior to whites, whether they were enslaved or free, and were given few rights.

In other words, Taney argued that the writers of the Constitution did not intend to include black Americans when they used the word "citizen," and therefore blacks had none of the rights guaranteed by the Constitution, including the right to sue in courts. "They had for more than a century before been regarded as beings of an inferior order, and altogether unfit to associate with the white race, either in social or political relations," Taney wrote. "They had no rights which the white man was bound to respect. . . . A negro of the African race was regarded . . . as an article of property."

Taney's decision overlooked a number of facts. Although most white Americans probably did not question whether slavery was morally right at the time the Constitution was written, the issue was not as straightforward as Taney believed. Even Thomas Jefferson, the nation's third president and the owner of many slaves himself, often expressed his doubts about slavery. "There is nothing I would not sacrifice to a practicable plan of abolishing every vestige of this moral and political depravity," Jefferson once wrote in a letter.

Justice
Roger Taney

Taney also overlooked the fact that several states had abolished slavery before the Constitution was written in 1787, including Connecticut, Massachusetts, Pennsylvania, and Rhode Island. By the end of the 1700s, New Hampshire, New York, and Vermont had also banned slavery. In some northern states, black men had the right to vote, and in many states they had the right to own property, with some even becoming quite wealthy. Taney's argument also ignored the fact that the Constitution did not specifically say that only whites were eligible to be citizens. Despite this history, Taney concluded that "Dred Scott was not a citizen of Missouri within the meaning of the Constitution of the United States, and not entitled as such to sue in its courts."

After the Civil War, Congress had passed the Fourteenth Amendment to the Constitution to make clear that blacks could be citizens. "All persons born or naturalized in the United States, and subject to the jurisdiction thereof, are citizens of the United States and of the State wherein they reside," the Amendment began. In other words, everyone—black or white, male or female—born in the United States was automatically an American citizen.

But even with the issue of citizenship for black Americans settled, another passage in the Amendment would turn out to be the subject of much debate: "No State shall make or enforce any law which shall abridge the privileges of immunities of citizens of the United States; nor shall any State deprive any person of life, liberty, or property, without due process of law; nor deny to any person within its jurisdiction the equal protection of the laws."

This passage seemed to mean that individual states could not take away the citizenship rights of any person, black or white. But what did it mean to deprive a person of life, liberty, or property? How much protection would the courts offer?

Strangely, the first time the U.S. Supreme Court took up those questions, it was in a case that had nothing to do with race. Although the primary purpose of the Fourteenth Amendment was to protect the rights of black men and women, others realized that they might be able to benefit from the Amendment as well. In 1873, the Supreme Court issued a ruling in a group of cases called the *Slaughter House* cases. A group of butchers in Louisiana—all of whom were white—sued the state to try to overturn a law that required all businesses where animal butchering took place to be located in spots where the waste would not run into the Mississippi River. It was feared that otherwise, the river could end up polluted by the animal waste. The butchers claimed that the law was unconstitutional under the Fourteenth Amendment because it took away their right to conduct business in certain locations.

In an important decision, five of the nine Supreme Court justices ruled against the butchers. Although the case did not involve race, it set an important precedent for future cases. The opinion of the majority of the justices stated that the Fourteenth Amendment had very specific purposes and should not be interpreted to mean that it had brought about any major changes regarding the laws that states could pass.

Ten years later, the Supreme Court issued a ruling that related directly to the rights of black Americans. In 1875, during Reconstruction, Congress had passed the Civil Rights Act, which required integration of public places and public transportation. Businesses would not be able to exclude blacks because of their race. In 1883, however, the Supreme Court declared that law unconstitutional. Congress could only guarantee political rights, such as voting, the Court ruled. It could not require public places to allow equal access to blacks and whites.

The Citizens' Committee and its lawyers knew that convincing the Supreme Court to rule that the Separate Car Act was unconstitutional would be difficult. It was not always easy for them to remain optimistic. Louis Martinet had made personal sacrifices in order to help lead the effort. Rather than focusing on trying to make money, he spent his time publishing a newspaper that he knew would never give him much of a financial return.

At times, Martinet grew frustrated with the struggle. It helped to have Tourgée on his side, as the men had become friends. In a letter written to Tourgée in July 1892, Martinet expressed his doubts that the Plessy case would turn out well. "The fight is a hard one; it is discouraging sometimes," he wrote. He wondered why he persisted in the battle against discrimination. "What have I to gain in fighting this battle? Like you, I have asked myself this question a thousand times. Certainly I gain nothing, but spend time, labor & money in it. There would be no doubt that if I turn my attention to, or put my energies in professional or some private pursuits I would get along much better in this world. Yes, why do I do it? I want no political influence, no prestige, no office. Like you, I believe I do it because I am built that way."

While waiting for the case to be heard by the Supreme Court, Martinet and other members of the Citizens' Committee also worked to turn the *Crusader*, which had been a weekly paper, into a daily paper. Citizens of New Orleans could subscribe for a year for $5.50. Martinet and Rodolphe Desdunes did much of the editing of the paper. Tourgée also contributed articles. The paper spoke out against discrimination in the hope that it might help turn public opinion.

Below: The interior of the Supreme Court of the United States circa 1894

Right: The actual court ruling of Dred Scott. On its way to the United States Supreme Court, the *Dred Scott* case grew in scope and significance as slavery became the single most explosive issue in American politics. By the time the case reached the high court, it had come to have enormous political implications for the entire nation.
On March 6, 1857, Chief Justice Roger B. Taney read the majority opinion of the Court, which stated that black people were not citizens of the United States and, therefore, could not expect any protection from the federal government or the courts; the opinion also stated that Congress had no authority to ban slavery from a federal territory. The decision of *Scott v. Sandford*, considered by legal scholars to be the worst ever rendered by the Supreme Court, was overturned by the Thirteenth and Fourteenth amendments to the Constitution, which abolished slavery and declared all persons born in the United States to be citizens of the United States.

No. 7.

Dred Scott　　　Pl'ff in Er

vs

John F. A. Sandford

In error to the Circuit Court of the
United States for the District of
Missouri. —

This cause came on to be
heard on the transcript of the record
from the Circuit Court of the United
States for the District of Missouri and
was argued by counsel — On Consider-
ation whereof, it is now here ordered
and adjudged by this court that the
judgment of the said Circuit Court
in this cause be and the same is
hereby reversed for the want of jurisdiction in that Court, and that this
cause be and the same is hereby
remanded to the said Circuit Court
with directions to dismiss the case
for the want of jurisdiction in that
Court. —

Jr. M. Ch. Ju. Taney
6th March 1857.

Martinet and Tourgée continued to discuss strategy in the Plessy case. Although they were eager to have their day in court, Tourgée knew that the Supreme Court might be unlikely to rule in their favor, so he hoped to put off the case for as long as possible. Supreme Court justices are appointed by the president to lifetime terms. That means that there are only openings on the Court when one justice retires or dies. Tourgée thought that if it took a long time for the case to be heard by the Court, in the meantime some of the justices who probably would rule against them might retire and be replaced by justices more likely to rule in their favor.

Tourgée also hoped to get the rest of the country on their side. "If we can get the ear of the Country, and argue the matter fully *before the people first*, we may incline the wavering to fall on our side when the matter comes up," Tourgée wrote to Martinet. Tourgée thought that, if most Americans supported equal rights for blacks, then the Supreme Court might be swayed by public opinion. "There are millions of the white people of the United States who believe in justice and equal right for the colored man," he wrote in a letter to Martinet.

Making the Case

Despite Tourgée's optimism, as the years passed the country did not seem to be growing any more sympathetic to the cause of equal rights for blacks. Instead, an economic recession that began in 1893 heightened racial tension as whites and blacks had to compete for jobs. In 1894, the Louisiana state legislature even strengthened the Separate Car Act by requiring that the waiting rooms at railroad stations also be segregated, not just the railroad cars.

For most white Americans, it was taken for granted that they were superior, both socially and intellectually, to blacks. The idea that the races were equal was not taken very seriously by most whites. One white Southern senator, John Tyler Morgan, wrote in 1890, for example, that "the inferiority of the negro race, as compared with the white race, is so essentially true, and so obvious, that, to assume it in argument, cannot be justly attributed to prejudice." In other words, believing that blacks were inferior did not make someone racist, it was simply the way things were, he believed. Morgan also argued that it actually harmed blacks to give them the right to vote, as they would either be taken advantage of by politicians or they would use their political power to get revenge on the whites who had enslaved them.

In the nineteenth century there were also many people who tried to use scientific reasoning to explain differences between blacks and whites. The German immigrant Frederick Hoffman used techniques developed by social scientists to argue that whites were intellectually superior to blacks, as well as to all other races. These arguments provided scientific language to confirm what most whites already wanted to believe—that there was little that could be done for black Americans.

Not all white Americans subscribed to such a prejudiced view of black Americans. Even before the Civil War, a few whites had fought against slavery and, in some cases, even for racial equality. After the end of the war, some Republican Congressmen who developed Reconstruction plans to help the freed slaves strongly believed that blacks could flourish if given a chance.

Just as whites disagreed about the place of blacks in American society, so, too, did some black Americans have different views of the best way for blacks to gain equal rights. One of the most famous, and outspoken, black Americans was Booker T. Washington, who had been born a slave in 1856 but became an important educator and leader. Washington gained his freedom with millions of other slaves at the end of the Civil War. He worked hard to learn to read and write, and eventually he attended the Hampton Institute, a college for blacks students.

Booker T. Washington

In the 1880s, Washington turned the Tuskegee Institute, a school for blacks in Alabama, into the best-known black school in the country. At the Institute, Washington stressed the importance of teaching students to learn skilled manual labor, such as agriculture, cooking, and building. He believed that if blacks could become an essential part of the Southern economy by succeeding in these manual trades, then they would eventually be able to gain social equality.

Washington had made his way upward in society through hard work; he even titled his autobiography *Up from Slavery*. And he believed that, by working hard at manual labor, other blacks would also be able to achieve success. In 1895, at a large exposition in Atlanta, Georgia, Washington gave a famous speech in which he discussed how blacks could become an

A 1902 photograph of a history class at the Tuskegee Institute in Tuskegee, Alabama

accepted part of society. "Our greatest danger is that in the great leap from slavery to freedom we may overlook the fact that the masses of us are to live by the production of our hands," he declared. He said it was more important for blacks to become successful farmers and laborers than to pursue higher education at universities.

Washington believed that black men and women should try to prove that they deserved equal rights by working their way up in society slowly. It was not necessary at first to be considered the social equals of whites, he argued, as long as blacks were given the chance to succeed economically. In one famous speech he gave in Atlanta in 1895, he reassured white listeners in his audience that he did not think it was necessary for blacks and whites to live equally side by side. "The wisest among my race understand that the agitation of questions of social equality is the extremest of folly," he said. "In all things that are purely social we can be as separate as the fingers, yet one as the hand in all things essential to mutual progress." So at the same time that Plessy, Martinet, and other blacks in New Orleans were working to end segregation, Washington was conceding that segregation might not be such a bad thing in some situations.

Washington did realize, however, that blacks faced many obstacles to learning trades and being accepted by whites. In his speech in Atlanta, he reminded the whites in the audience that the labor of blacks had built the railroads and cleared the fields of the South. If whites would just give blacks a chance by offering them work, Washington said, "you and your families will be surrounded by the most patient, faithful, law-abiding, and unresentful people that the world has ever seen."

The arguments Washington made gained him quite a bit of fame, including the chance later to meet with President

Theodore Roosevelt in the White House. Many black leaders, however, strongly disagreed with Washington's views. After all, without equal rights it could be hard for blacks to make the kind of economic progress that Washington thought they should. Violence against blacks in the South seemed to show that it would take more than goodwill on the part of blacks to make progress. Without the protection of the federal government, which had removed federal troops from the South in 1877, whites had been able to keep blacks from using their political rights, such as the right to vote.

Another prominent black man, W. E. B. Du Bois, took a very different point of view from Washington. Born in 1868, Du Bois was much younger than Washington, and he was from Massachusetts rather than the South. In 1895, he became the first black American to earn a Ph D from Harvard University. Keeping blacks and whites separate, he argued, would only make racial prejudice persist, and it would be impossible for blacks to make economic progress without political rights, such as the right to vote.

Whatever the opinion of most Americans, it would be up to just a few men to decide Plessy's fate. In 1896, Plessy's case was finally scheduled to be heard by the Supreme Court. By now, Martinet and the rest of the Citizens' Committee had enlisted the help of other attorneys as well as Tourgée and Walker. The legal team had two chances to make its case. Tourgée would argue in front of the Supreme Court on Monday, April 13. He and the rest of the legal team would also submit written legal briefs to the Court that stated the case.

Privately, Tourgée was concerned that they had little chance of winning the case. In letters to Martinet, he admitted that he was worried that at least five of the nine justices would almost surely rule against them. That would be all it would take to lose the decision, as whatever the majority of

The 1896 Supreme Court Justices
that decided Plessy's fate

the justices decided would determine the outcome. All nine members of the Supreme Court were white men. One, Justice John Marshall Harlan, was from Kentucky. Although he was the only Southerner on the Court, he was also the most likely to side with Plessy. During the Civil War, Harlan had joined the Union Army. As a member of the Supreme Court, Harlan had a history of supporting the rights of blacks, which made Tourgée hopeful that Harlan, at least, might rule in their favor.

Tourgée had only half an hour to make his case before the Court on April 13. During his argument, he tried to convince the justices that the Fourteenth Amendment should be interpreted broadly. The Amendment, he argued, was not just intended to make blacks citizens: it was also intended to ensure that they were treated equally by each individual state.

Justice John Marshall Harlan

The written arguments submitted by Plessy's lawyers took several different approaches to the issue. One argument was that a person's race was not always obvious. Therefore, it could be difficult for a conductor on a railroad car to be able to determine quickly whether a person was black or white, and it should not be left up to a single employee to make that decision. There was no clear way for a conductor to be sure of a person's race, they argued. If there was no obvious way to know a person's race, how could railroad companies be expected to enforce the law? Also, the law did not clearly define what it meant to be black or white. Should a passenger such as Plessy, who had both white and black grandparents and whose skin was very light, automatically be classified as black?

The legal team also relied on both the Thirteenth and Fourteenth Amendments to make its case. The Thirteenth Amendment had abolished slavery. "Neither slavery nor involuntary servitude, except as a punishment for crime whereof the party shall have been duly convicted, shall exist within the United States," the Amendment stated. Plessy's lawyers argued that enforcing segregation of blacks and whites in public places was one of the features of slavery and that therefore the law was unconstitutional under the Thirteenth Amendment.

The Fourteenth Amendment, they argued, also required a holding in Plessy's favor. It declared that everyone—black and white—was equal before the law, so laws like the Separate Car Act that created distinctions between people based on race were unconstitutional. Tourgée and Plessy's other lawyers believed that the Fourteenth Amendment had created a new meaning of citizenship. They argued that the federal government now had the final authority in what it meant to be a citizen and that states could not be allowed to discriminate against individuals based on race.

The lawyers for the state of Louisiana, Milton Cunningham and Alexander Porter Morse, made their own arguments in support of the Separate Car Act. They claimed that it was not difficult for a railroad conductor to tell the difference between a black person and a white person, so the law could easily be enforced by a railroad conductor. They also argued that the law did not conflict with the Thirteenth and Fourteenth Amendments for several reasons. First, the law did not make anyone a slave, so the Thirteenth Amendment could not apply to the case. Second, the law treated everyone equally—blacks were banned from sitting in the cars reserved for whites, and whites were banned from sitting in the cars reserved for blacks. Therefore, the law did not discriminate. The Fourteenth Amendment, they said, did not guarantee that public places would be integrated. The two lawyers also cited earlier rulings made by the Supreme Court in support of their case, such as the 1883 ruling that struck down the Civil Rights Act.

Once the hearings were over, there was nothing left for Plessy, Tourgée, or any of the members of the Citizens' Committee to do but wait. The suspense did not last too long. One month later, on May 18, 1896, the Supreme Court issued its ruling.

8

The Opinion
of the Court

In the end, only eight men ruled on the case that would help determine the future of race relations in the United States. Although the Supreme Court had nine justices, one had removed himself from the case. If the remaining eight justices decided that the law was unconstitutional, it might contribute to a more racially integrated society. If they decided to allow the law to stand, they would be putting the weight of the highest court in the country behind segregation based on skin color.

Of the eight justices, seven ruled to uphold the Separate Car Act, deciding that it was constitutional. Only one justice, John Marshall Harlan, disagreed. The law could remain in effect. Four years after Homer Plessy was arrested for boarding the wrong railroad car, his case would finally proceed.

Justice Henry Billings Brown wrote the decision for the seven justices who ruled to uphold the law. Brown was from a wealthy Massachusetts family. Like many lawyers at the time, he did not have a law degree, but he had studied law at both Yale and Harvard. Also like many wealthy Northerners, during the Civil War he paid for a substitute to serve in the Union army so that he would not have to. The practice of paying for substitutes allowed men who had been drafted to avoid serving in the army, if they could afford to pay a fee of three hundred dollars or find someone to substitute for them. He had served on the Supreme Court since 1890, and, although he was from the North, he had shown little sympathy for racial equality in earlier decisions.

Justice Henry
Billings Brown

Brown began his opinion by dismissing Tourgée's argument that the Thirteenth Amendment, which banned slavery, applied to Plessy's case. Brown agreed with the lawyers for the state of Louisiana that it was clear that the Thirteenth Amendment did not apply because the Separate Car Act did not force anyone into slavery. All it did, he wrote, was distinguish between people of different races. "A statute which implies merely a legal distinction between the white and colored races—a distinction which is founded in the color of the two races and which must always exist so long as white men are distinguished from the other race by color—has no tendency to destroy the legal equality of the two races, or to reestablish a state of involuntary servitude," he wrote. In other words, Brown believed that there were real and obvious differences between blacks and whites, and it was not unconstitutional simply to recognize those differences. Forcing people to ride in certain railroad cars because of their race did not make them slaves.

Brown also discussed the argument that the law was unconstitutional under the Fourteenth Amendment, which he thought was a more complicated issue. Certainly, he wrote, Congress did intend when it passed the Amendment to ensure that blacks and whites were treated equally under the law. But, he continued, the Amendment "could not have been intended to abolish distinctions based upon color, or to enforce social, as distinguished from political equality." Brown and his fellow justices, like most white Americans, believed strongly that there were basic differences between blacks and whites, and so it was unthinkable that an Amendment to the Constitution could make the two races equal. Guaranteeing the right to vote was one thing, but it was hard for Brown to imagine that when Congress passed the Fourteenth Amendment it had intended to guarantee that blacks and whites would be social equals.

In an earlier decision, the Supreme Court had struck down a West Virginia law that required all jurors to be white men over the age of twenty-one, because that took away the political right of blacks to serve on juries. But the justices believed that Plessy's case was about social rights, not political rights. Brown wrote that laws that prohibited interracial marriage or that segregated railroad cars, or other public places such as schools, did not take away any rights from blacks because there were still railroad cars available to them. One mistake in the argument made by Plessy's lawyers, Brown decided, was the assumption that segregation "stamps the colored race with a badge of inferiority." There was no reason for blacks to think that they were being discriminated against, because whites were also banned from riding in cars reserved for blacks. Of course, the justices did not take into account the fact that the cars reserved for whites were often in better condition than those reserved for blacks, so the accommodations were not really equal.

Another mistake in Tourgée's argument, according to Brown, was the belief that a law could create social equality between blacks and whites. "Legislation is powerless to eradicate racial instincts or to abolish distinctions based upon physical differences," Brown wrote. Brown believed that there were significant differences between blacks and whites, and no law could make those differences go away. "If one race be inferior to the other socially, the Constitution of the United States cannot put them on the same plane," he wrote.

Justice John Marshall Harlan was the only justice to disagree with the majority, and he wrote a dissenting opinion to explain his reasoning. Given Harlan's background, it is somewhat surprising that he had become the strongest supporter of the rights of blacks on the Supreme Court. He had been born into a wealthy family in Kentucky. His family, like many successful white families in Kentucky, owned slaves. As the Civil War approached, however, Harlan worked to prevent Kentucky from seceding, and when the war began, he served in the Union army. He had never been a supporter of rights for blacks, but after the war, his views began to change. By the time Plessy's case made its way to the Supreme Court, he was the only justice that Tourgée and Martinet were confident would rule in their favor.

Harlan began his dissenting opinion by explaining that railroad employees had no right to know whether a passenger was black or white, so they certainly should not be the ones to determine a person's race. He also disagreed with the majority's opinion of the meaning of the Thirteenth and Fourteenth Amendments. He explained that the Thirteenth Amendment meant not only to abolish slavery, but also to take away any burdens that could be seen as a sign of slavery, such as forcing one group of people to sit apart from others because of race. He believed that the Fourteenth Amendment also prevented this type of discrimination. "If a white man and a black man choose to occupy the same public conveyance on a public highway, it is their right to do so," he wrote.

Brown's opinion for the majority of the Court had found that the Separate Car Act did not discriminate against anyone because it treated everyone equally. Harlan pointed out, however, that the law was obviously intended to keep black passengers out of white railroad cars, and not the other way around. He also recognized that the cars might not be equal.

If a state government could require separate railroad cars, Harlan asked, how far could a state go in enforcing segregation, and what could it use as the basis of segregation? Could it require blacks and whites to walk on opposite sides of the street? Could it force blacks and whites to sit separately in courthouses or other public places? Or could a state enforce discrimination on other grounds, such as religion? It would make just as much sense, he argued, for a state to be allowed to pass a law requiring Catholics and Protestants to ride in different railroad cars. Once the Supreme Court allowed states to pass discriminatory laws, how far would it allow states to go?

Harlan agreed with Brown that people of different races were not necessarily equal, but he argued that they should be treated equally under the law. If whites were superior to blacks, he wrote, it was unlikely that striking down laws such as the Separate Car Act would put an end to that superiority. "In the eye of the law, there is in this country no superior, dominant, ruling class of citizens," he wrote. "The law regards man as man, and takes no account of his surroundings or of his color when his civil rights as guaranteed by the supreme law of the land are involved."

Although Harlan believed that blacks and whites should be treated equally, he did have his own prejudices about race. He pointed out that under the Separate Car Act, a black person could not ride in a railroad car with a white person, but a Chinese person would be allowed in the white car. The Chinese, he wrote, were believed to be so different from whites that they were not even allowed to become citizens. Blacks, on the other hand, had risked their lives during the Civil War to fight for the Union.

Harlan concluded that the majority of the Court had made a very unfortunate unwise ruling. One day, he wrote, it would be viewed as negatively as the *Dred Scott* decision. He believed that the lives and interests of blacks and whites could not be separated and that everyone would suffer if the Court allowed legal segregation to continue. The majority of the Court had ruled that laws enforcing segregation would help avoid violence between blacks and whites. But Harlan found that by keeping people separated simply because of race, it was more likely for hate to grow between blacks and whites, possibly leading to worse violence and misunderstanding in the future.

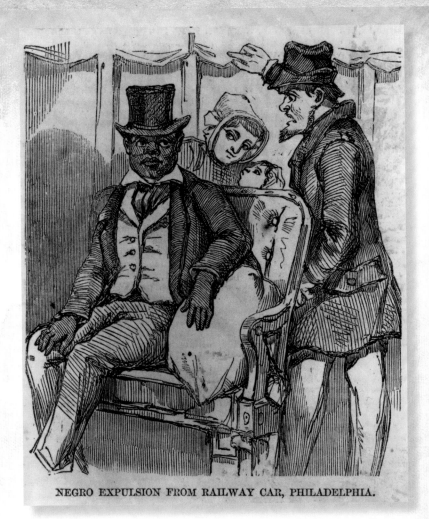

NEGRO EXPULSION FROM RAILWAY CAR, PHILADELPHIA.

An illustration published in the September 27, 1856, issue of the *Illustrated London News*. The illustration depicts a white man ordering a free black man to leave a whites-only car.

Despite Harlan's passionate opinion, the opinion of the other seven justices ruled the day. The Separate Car Act was allowed to stand. The decision of the Supreme Court set a precedent that became known as "separate but equal." This meant that laws that enforced segregation were constitutional as long as everyone had access to equal accommodations. Black and white children could be required to attend different schools as long as the schools were equal. In reality, however, accommodations for blacks and whites were rarely equal. In the case of education, for example, schools for white children were likely to be in much better condition and have much better supplies than schools for black children.

The Supreme Court's ruling did not attract as much attention at the time as it would later, but many newspapers across the country did comment on the decision. The New Orleans *Daily Picayune* praised the decision. "If all rights were common as well as equal, there would be practically no such thing as private property, private life, or social distinctions," an editorial in the paper stated. "This would be absolute socialism, in which the individual would be extinguished in the vast mass of human beings."

Other papers throughout the South celebrated the decision as well, believing that it upheld the rights of individual states to regulate themselves. "Some colored people make themselves so disagreeable on the cars that their conduct leads white men to ponder the question whether such a law as that of Louisiana is not needed in all the Southern States," an editorial in a Richmond, Virginia, paper stated.

Others disagreed with the decision, including a paper published in Rochester, New York. "The announcement of this decision will be received by thoughtful and fair-minded people with disapproval and regret," the paper argued. "It is not in harmony with the principles of this republic or with the spirit of our time. . . . It puts the official stamp of the highest court in the country upon the miserable doctrine that several millions of American citizens are of an inferior race and unfit to mingle with citizens of other races." An editorial in a black Kansas paper, the *Weekly Blade*, praised Justice Harlan's courage. "Justice Harlan was the only one on that bench with enough grit in him to utter a protest against this damnable outrage," it stated.

The black novelist Charles Chestnutt, a friend of Tourgée, wrote of the decision that it was "a clear and definite approval of the recognition by State laws, of color distinctions, something which had theretofore been avoided in civil rights cases. It establishes racial caste in the United States as firmly as though it were established by act of Congress." Chestnutt worried that the decision would set a precedent that would stand for many years and that would encourage other states to pass laws that enforced strict segregation as well. The fears of Tourgée and Martinet that a loss would set back the movement for equal rights seemed to have come to pass.

Chesnutt's concerns of future segregation would come true as whites and blacks were still segregated in the 1950s.

For Homer Plessy, the decision did not significantly change his life. He appeared before Judge Ferguson in New Orleans again, this time to plead guilty and pay a twenty-five dollar fine, after which he returned to work. He continued to live in New Orleans until his death in 1925.

Albion Tourgée was devastated by the decision. In the months after the end of the case, he worked for the political campaigns of Republican candidates, including presidential candidate William McKinley, who was elected president later in the fall of 1896. But Tourgée found himself feeling increasingly hopeless about race relations in the United States. He hoped to be named to a diplomatic position in France. When the opportunity came, not long after McKinley's election, Tourgée was relieved to leave behind his country at least for a while. He had always thought that, in the end, the belief of white Americans in liberty and justice would lead them to allow black Americans to become full members of American society. But in the years following the case, his hope and stature in American public life began to fade.

Before long, even Tourgée's literary fame gradually diminished. A new edition of his popular book *A Fool's Errand* had been issued in 1894, but it no longer sold well. Instead, in the late 1800s and early 1900s, books that took a different perspective on Reconstruction began to gain popularity. The novelist Thomas Dixon's books *The Leopard's Spots* and *The Clansmen* depicted white southerners as victims of blacks and northern politicians during Reconstruction. The movie *The Birth of a Nation*, based on Dixon's book *The Clansmen*, became an early blockbuster success when it was released in 1915, and it helped to shape the way white Americans remembered the years after the Civil War. For years to come, many white historians would argue that Reconstruction had been a failure because of the federal government and corrupt black politicians, not because of the violence used by some whites to prevent blacks from exercising their rights as citizens.

For the most part, white Americans in both the North and South were ready to overlook discrimination against blacks. It had been more than thirty years since the end of the Civil War, and there were other matters gaining public attention. Meanwhile, in the South, the Plessy decision helped create a society that was strictly divided by race. Soon almost every facet of public life was affected by segregation. There were not just different railroad cars for blacks and whites, there were also different rest rooms, cemeteries, schools, parks, and even water fountains.

In 1898, Louisiana created a new state constitution that undid much of the progress that had been made during Reconstruction. Schools were now segregated. The constitution also made it much harder for blacks to register to vote, in effect taking away the right guaranteed by the Fifteenth Amendment. Anyone who wanted to register to vote had to pay a poll tax and have completed some education in order to be eligible to vote. But those who had been entitled to vote before 1867, when only whites were allowed to vote, were allowed to continue voting without paying the poll tax or meeting other qualifications. As a result, the number of blacks in Louisiana who took part in elections quickly plummeted. From 1896 to 1904, the number of registered black voters dropped from more than 130,000 to less than 1,500. For decades to come, whites in Louisiana and other Southern states dominated local elections by preventing blacks from exercising their right to vote, even in states where blacks made up a majority of the population. Even in 1940, there were fewer than one thousand registered black voters in Louisiana.

There were also hundreds of lynchings—or organized murders—of blacks in the decades around the time of the Plessy decision. Southern states made it difficult or impossible for

Grant.

Dulany. Duglass, Revels.

PUBLISHED & PRINTED BY

Entered according to act of Congress in the year 1870 by Th. Kelly in the Office of the Librarian

THE FIFTEENTH AME

1 *Reading Emancipation Proclamation*
2 *Life Liberty and Independence*
3 *We Unite the Bonds of Fellowship.*
4 *Our Charter of Rights the Holy Scriptures.*

5 *Education will prove the Equality the Races.*
6 *Liberty Protects the Mariage Alter.*
7 *Celebration of Fifteenth Amendment May 19th 1870*
8 *The Ballot Box is open to us.*

9 *Our represensive Sits i*
10 *The Holy Ordinance.*
11 *Freedom unites the F*
12 *We will protect our Cou*

The Fifteenth Amendment, an 1870 print celebrating the passage of the Fifteenth Amendment to the United States Constitution in February 1870 and the advancements that African Americans had made as a result of the Civil War

blacks to serve on juries, which meant that crimes against blacks by whites often went unpunished because all-white juries would not convict whites of those crimes. The integrated schools of the 1870s in New Orleans also became just a distant memory, as many black children were not even able to attend school. Less than half of the black children in Louisiana were enrolled in school in 1915, compared to about 79 percent of white children.

9

A Separate and Unequal Society

In 1903, W. E. B. Du Bois published the book *The Souls of Black Folk*, in which he predicted that "The problem of the Twentieth Century is the problem of the color-line." Du Bois meant that the question of how blacks and whites would live together in the United States would affect every aspect of life. He turned out to be correct about the importance of this question, and one reason for the persistence of racism was the decision of the Supreme Court to allow segregation to continue in the case of *Plessy v. Ferguson*.

For almost sixty years, the decision in *Plessy v. Ferguson* provided a legal basis for segregation on the basis of race. Throughout that period, however, some stalwart Americans continued working to bring segregation to an end. In 1909, a group of civil rights activists formed the National Association for the Advancement of Colored People (NAACP) to fight against segregation and discrimination. The NAACP used legal challenges to try to overturn discriminatory laws, just as Martinet, Tourgée, and the Citizens' Committee had attempted to do in Louisiana in the 1890s.

One of the leaders of the NAACP was a black lawyer named Thurgood Marshall. He traveled around the South in the 1930s and 1940s to document examples of discrimination and to represent in court blacks who had been accused of crimes. And when the NAACP decided to challenge *Plessy v. Ferguson* in the courts—to try to overturn the decision written by Henry Billings Brown—Marshall helped lead the way.

The NAACP believed that the most likely way to succeed in challenging the precedent set by *Plessy v. Ferguson* was to focus on public education. After all, the decision in the case had stated that it was fine to require segregation, but the accommodations for blacks and whites had to be equal. In the first half of the twentieth century, it was clear that the education provided to black students and white students was far from equal. States with segregated school systems spent much more on schools for white children than schools for black children. Black teachers were not paid as well as white teachers. Even the schools themselves could be very different, as black schools were more likely to be run down and in need of repair.

Before challenging the legality of segregation, however, the NAACP filed a handful of lawsuits meant to force states to live up to the "equal" part of "separate but equal." In 1938, the organization won a case before the Supreme Court that did just that. A college graduate in Missouri named Lloyd Gaines applied to the University of Missouri law school but was rejected because he was black. The state of Missouri agreed to pay to send Gaines to attend law school in another state, but instead Gaines and the NAACP sued, arguing that the

Thurgood Marshall in 1957

state either had to admit Gaines to the University of Missouri or create a law school for black students. The Supreme Court sided with Gaines and the NAACP. The ruling was important because it meant that all states had to do more to provide equal educational opportunities.

As a result of this decision and other legal victories, some southern states did begin to spend more on education for black students, including in Louisiana. In 1940, Louisiana spent only sixteen dollars per student each year on education for black students. By 1955, the state had increased spending to $116 for each black student.

Still, that amount was less than what Louisiana spent on white students, and throughout the South education for blacks continued to be less than equal. Even with the progress that had been made, it seemed unlikely that conditions would ever truly be equal as long as segregation persisted. The NAACP's next step was to challenge the legality of segregation. Led by Thurgood Marshall, the organization decided to go to court to argue that segregated schools could never be equal, and that the doctrine of "separate but equal" should be overturned.

As a result of lawsuits filed by the NAACP, the Supreme Court again took up the issue of segregation, this time in 1954 in the case *Brown v. Board of Education of Topeka, Kansas*. The *Brown* case actually consisted of four cases from four different states, all involving the segregation of schools. Black children in each of the states were provided public education, but they wanted to attend white schools. This time, instead of arguing only that the schools for blacks and whites should be equal, Thurgood Marshall and the NAACP argued before the Supreme Court that "separate" could never be "equal," and therefore the precedent set by *Plessy v. Ferguson* should be overturned.

On May 17, 1954, the Supreme Court issued its decision. It unanimously ruled against segregation and reversed the precedent set by Plessy's 1896 case. "In each of the cases . . . a three-judge federal district court denied relief to the plaintiffs on the so-called 'separate but equal' doctrine announced by this Court in *Plessy v. Ferguson*," the justices stated in their decision. "Under that doctrine, equality of treatment is accorded when the races are provided substantially equal facilities, even though these facilities be separate."

The Supreme Court agreed with the NAACP that segregation itself created inequality. Separating children based only on race "generates a feeling of inferiority as to their status in the community that may affect their hearts and minds in a way unlikely ever to be undone," the court wrote. It also explained that laws separating people based on race were generally understood to mark black people as inferior to whites. Therefore, the court ruled, the precedent of "separate but equal" could not stand. The decision was important because it declared that even if facilities were equal—that is, even if the schools that black and white children attended had equal funding and supplies—segregation was still unconstitutional. "Does segregation of children in public schools solely on the basis of race, even though the physical facilities and other 'tangible' factors may be equal, deprive the children of the minority group of equal educational opportunities?" the court asked. "We believe that it does."

Even this decision, however, would not mark the end of segregation, either in public schools or in other aspects of life. Not long after the ruling was issued, many congressmen from southern states signed a document condemning the Supreme Court's decision. At the time of the ruling, twenty-one states had segregated public schools. Three years after the decision, fewer than seven hundred of the 3,000 school districts in the South that should have been desegregated had actually made any progress in doing so. The decades of segregation allowed by the decision in *Plessy v. Ferguson* had created a society where, to many, it seemed natural to have whites and blacks segregated in all areas of public life. Those who had been born in the South and grown up there had trouble imagining any other way of life.

A test of the Supreme Court's ruling came in the fall of 1957 in Little Rock, Arkansas. Nine black high school students were set to become the first black students at the city's Central High School. The governor of Arkansas, Orval Faubus, declared that he opposed desegregation. The black students were scheduled to begin classes on September 4. But when they arrived at the school, they found that Faubus had ordered the state's National Guard troops to prevent the students from entering. One of the black students, fifteen-year-old Elizabeth Eckford, twice tried to enter the school's doors. Both times, the National Guardsmen blocked her way.

The situation changed little for the next three weeks, as the troops continued to guard the school's entrances. Finally, on September 20, Faubus withdrew the troops. On Monday morning, September 23, eight of the black students entered the school. A large crowd of angry white men and women gathered outside the school. In the middle of the school day, the city's mayor and school superintendent were so worried about the safety of the black students that they had them leave secretly to avoid any violence from the mob outside. Two days later, President Dwight Eisenhower ordered federal troops to the school to protect the black students and to allow desegregation to proceed. Once again, just as during Reconstruction, it had taken intervention by the federal government to ensure that the law would be followed.

In New Orleans and all of Louisiana, as in the rest of the South, it had become hard to imagine an end to a segregated society, but there had been some changes. The city's libraries, which had long barred blacks from entering, became integrated in 1953. In 1954 and 1955, a few black students were admitted to colleges in Louisiana. The state's public school system, however, remained segregated. As soon as the *Brown* decision was handed down by the Supreme Court, Louisiana's state legislature passed a number of bills criticizing the decision and finding ways to get around it. One law, for example, declared that only segregated public schools could receive funding from the state. The state legislature even created a committee whose job was to find ways to avoid integration, called the Joint Legislative Committee to Maintain Segregation.

The New Orleans school board proved to be even more stubborn than Orval Faubus in Little Rock. By 1960, the board had not made any effort to integrate the city's schools. Instead, it used legal appeals to delay the need to integrate.

A 1959 photograph of a rally at the Arkansas state capitol protesting the integration of Central High School in Little Rock

But in the spring of 1960, a judge ruled that the city must begin the process of desegregation the next fall. At that time, students entering first grade would be allowed to choose to attend either the closest all-white school or the closest all-black school. There were more black children in the city than white children, which meant that this ruling could lead to wide-spread integration. In response, the state legislature passed a bill that allowed the governor, Jimmie Davis, to close every public school in the entire state if any of the schools were inte-grated. As the new school year approached, some whites in the state became worried about what would happen to educa-tion in the state if all the public schools were closed, and they began an effort to keep the schools open, although they did not necessarily support integration.

Finally, the school board came up with its own integration plan, which the courts approved. In November, black students would be allowed to apply for a transfer to an all-white school. Not every student would be approved, giving the school board the ability to minimize the number of schools that became inte-grated. Out of 137 black applicants, only five were approved. When one student dropped out of the process, only four first-grade girls were left to begin the integration of New Orleans's schools for the first time since the *Plessy* decision.

As November 14 approached, the city and state were on edge. Ten days before the day set for integration, the state leg-islature approved a law that created a committee that would take control of the schools in New Orleans to block integra-tion. When the courts and the federal government took action to allow integration to proceed, the state legislature declared Monday, November 14, a school holiday.

When the fourteenth arrived, state policemen went to the city's schools to tell the schools' principles that there was a hol-iday. At every school, however, the principles kept the schools open at the request of the school board. Three of the four black girls were attending the same school, and they were escorted there by federal marshals. The fourth girl was brought to a different school, where she was the only black student. White crowds gathered outside to protest the schools, but there was no violence, and it seemed that integration might be allowed to proceed.

Over the next two days, however, the protests grew larger and more violent. Only when the police doused the mobs with fire hoses did the protests subside. By November 16, almost all of the white students at the two integrated schools had been kept home in protest. Integration continued, but with the constant presence of angry whites outside the schools and few white students inside the schools. The next school year, a few more black students were admitted to schools that had previously only had white students.

Although most schools remained segregated, integration had slowly begun. The decision in the *Brown* case and the fight to enforce that decision finally put an end to legally sanctioned segregation. Almost seventy years after Homer Plessy sat in a segregated railroad car and refused to leave, the era of enforced segregation was coming to an end.

A 1955 photograph showing the integrated
Barnard School in Washington, D.C.

Timeline

1857   In the *Dred Scott* decision, Roger Taney finds that blacks are not United States citizens.

1860   November: Abraham Lincoln is elected president.

        December: South Carolina becomes the first state to secede from the Union.

1861   April: The Civil War begins.

1863   March: Homer Plessy is born.

1865   January: Congress passes the Thirteenth Amendment, which abolishes slavery in the United States.

        April: The Civil War comes to an end.

1866   Congress passes the Fourteenth Amendment to the Constitution.

1867   April: Blacks in New Orleans force the integration of streetcars.

1869   Congress passes the Fifteenth Amendment to the Constitution; when it is ratified in 1870, the Amendment gives black men the right to vote.

1877   Reconstruction comes to an end when the federal government withdraws troops from the South.

1883   The Supreme Court rules that the 1875 Civil Rights Act is unconstitutional.

1890   The Louisiana state legislature passes the Separate Car Act, requiring separate railroad cars for blacks and whites.

1891   September: A group of black men in New Orleans form the Citizens' Committee to Test the Constitutionality of the Separate Car Law.

1892   June 7: Homer Plessy is arrested after sitting in a first-class car on a train in New Orleans.

        October 28: Judge John Ferguson hears arguments about whether the case against Homer Plessy should proceed.

        November 18: Ferguson rules that the Separate Car Act is constitutional.

1896   May: The Supreme Court rules that the Separate Car Act is constitutional, allowing the case against Plessy to proceed and instituting the legal doctrine of "separate but equal."

1909   The National Association for the Advancement of Colored People (NAACP) is formed.

1954   May: The U.S. Supreme Court issues its ruling in the case of *Brown v. Board of Education of Topeka, Kansas*.

Sources

CHAPTER ONE: **A Very Short Train Ride**

p. 14,   "The sooner they drop . . ." Otto Olsen, ed., *The Thin Disguise* (New York: Humanities Press, 1967), 70-71.

CHAPTER TWO: **The Shadow of Slavery**

p. 18,   "I do not believe . . ." Elizabeth Cobbs Hoffman and Jon Gjerde, eds., *Major Problems in American History, Volume 1: To 1877* (Boston: Houghton Mifflin, 2006), 372.

p. 19,   "Free them . . ." Ibid., 373.

CHAPTER FOUR: **Integration and Segregation**

p. 39,   "Every man, no matter . . ." Ibid., 429.

CHAPTER FIVE: **A Slap in the Face**

p. 48,   "Citizenship is national . . ." Olsen, *The Thin Disguise*, 48.

p. 48,   "Among the many schemes . . ." Keith Weldon Medley, *We as Freemen: Plessy v. Ferguson* (Gretna, La.: Pelican Publishing Company, 2003), 116-7.

pp. 48-49, "A man that would . . ." Olsen, *The Thin Disguise*, 53.

CHAPTER SIX: **Challenging the Law**

pp. 63-64, "They had for more . . ." Hoffman and Gjerde, *Major Problems in American History*, 371.

p. 64,   "There is nothing . . ." William B. Parker and Jonas Viles, eds., *Letters and Addresses of Thomas Jefferson* (New York: A. Wessels Company, 1907), 245.

p. 65,   "Dred Scott was not . . ." Hoffman and Gjerde, *Major Problems in American History*, 371.

p. 67,   "The fight is a hard one . . ." Olsen, *The Thin Disguise*, 65.

p. 67,   "What have I to gain . . ." Ibid., 63-64.

p. 70,   "If we can get the ear . . ." Ibid., 79.

CHAPTER SEVEN: **Making the Case**

pp. 71-72,   "The inferiority . . ." Brook Thomas, ed., *Plessy v. Ferguson: A Brief History With Documents* (Boston: Bedford/St. Martin's, 1997), 68.

p. 75,   "Our greatest danger . . ." Ibid., 122.

p. 75,   "The wisest among my race . . ." Ibid., 124.

p. 75,   "you and your families . . ." Ibid., 122.

CHAPTER EIGHT: **The Opinion of the Court**

p. 83,   "A statute which implies . . ." Thomas, *Plessy v. Ferguson: A Brief History With Documents*, 43.

p. 83,   "could not have been intended . . ." Ibid., 44.

p. 84,   "stamps the colored race. . . Ibid., 51.

p. 84,   "Legislation is powerless . . ." Ibid.

p. 85,   "If a white man . . ." Ibid., 55.

p. 86,   "In the eye of the law . . ." Ibid., 57.

p. 88,   "If all rights were common . . ." Olsen, *The Thin Disguise*, 123.

p. 88,   "Some colored people . . ." Ibid., 127.

p. 88,   "The announcement of this decision . . ." Ibid., 124.

p. 88,   "Justice Harlan . . ." Ibid., 129.

p. 89,   "a clear and definite . . ." Thomas, *Plessy v. Ferguson: Brief History With Documents*, 155-156.

CHAPTER NINE: **A Separate and Unequal Society**

p. 95,   "The problem of the . . ." W. E. B. DuBois, *The Souls of Black Folk* (New York: Bantam Books, 1989), 10.

p. 99,   "In each of the cases . . ." *Brown v. Board of Education*, 347 U.S. 483 (1954), http://laws.findlaw.com/us/347/483.html.

p. 99,   "generates a feeling . . ." Ibid.

p. 99,   "Does segregation of children . . ." Ibid.

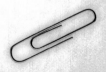

Bibliography

Blassingame, John W. *Black New Orleans, 1860-1880*. Chicago: University of Chicago Press, 1973.

Elliott, Mark. *Color-Blind Justice: Albion Tourgée and the Quest for Racial Equality from the Civil War to Plessy v. Ferguson*. New York: Oxford University Press, 2006.

Fireside, Harvey. *Separate and Unequal: Homer Plessy and the Supreme Court Decision That Legalized Racism*. New York: Carroll & Graf Publishers, 2004.

Fischer, Roger A. *The Segregation Struggle in Louisiana, 1862-77*. Urbana, Il.: University of Illinois Press, 1974.

Foner, Eric. *Reconstruction: America's Unfinished Revolution, 1863-1877*. New York: Harper & Row Publishers, 1988.

Hogue, James K. *Uncivil War: Five New Orleans Street Battles and the Rise and Fall of Radical Reconstruction*. Baton Rouge: Louisiana State University Press, 2006.

Medley, Keith Weldon. *We as Freemen: Plessy v. Ferguson*. Gretna, La.: Pelican Publishing Company, 2003.

Nystrom, Justin A. *New Orleans after the Civil War: Race, Politics, and a New Birth of Freedom*. Baltimore: The Johns Hopkins University Press, 2010.

Web sites

www.pbs.org/wnet/jimcrow/stories_events_plessy.html
   A short description of the *Plessy v. Ferguson* case as well as a video link.

www.ourdocuments.gov
   The *Plessy v. Ferguson* case is among the 100 Milestone Documents of American History featured on this site, compiled by the National Archives and Records Administration.

http://www.americaslibrary.gov/cgi-bin/page.cgi/ib/progress/plessy_1
   Learn more about the *Plessy v. Ferguson* case here on the Web site of the Library of Congress.

http://www.nola.com/news/index.ssf/2009/02/plessy_vs_ferguson_photo.htm
   A *Times-Picayune* newspaper article about the ancestors of Plessy and Ferguson unveiling a plaque to mark their ancestors' actions. Published February 11, 2009.

Index

Photo Credits

All images used in this book that are not in the public domain are credited in the listing that follows:

Cover:	Courtesy of Library of Congress
11:	Used under license from iStockphoto.com
23:	Courtesy of Library of Congress
30:	Courtesy of Library of Congress
45:	Courtesy of Library of Congress
87:	The Art Gallery Collection / Alamy
89:	AP Photo
97:	Courtesy of Library of Congress
101:	Courtesy of Library of Congress
104:	Courtesy of Library of Congress